Written by Gurj Bassi

Edited by Philippa Wingate
Designed by Button Group plc
Production by Joanne Rooke
Picture Research by Judith Palmer

Picture Acknowledgments

Front cover: Richard Young / Rex Features
Back cover: Justin Goff / cd:uk
Endpapers: David Fisher / LFI

Andy Butterton / PA / Empics: pages 22/23
Yui Mok / PA / Empics: pages 7, 9, 11, 13, 21, 26/27
Justin Goff / cd:uk: pages 2, 18, 44/45, 54/55
Rob Cable / LFI: page 29
Barry Clack / LFI: pages 30, 35
David Fisher / LFI: pages 14/15
Rex Features: pages 42, 50
Ray Tang / Rex Features: pages 46/47
Richard Young / Rex Features: pages 36/37

First published in Great Britain in 2005 by Buster Books,
an imprint of Michael O'Mara Books Limited,
9 Lion Yard, Tremadoc Road,
London SW4 7NQ

A CIP catalogue record for this book is available from the British Library.

ISBN : 1-905158-01-7

2 4 6 8 10 9 7 5 3 1
Printed and bound in Italy by L.E.G.O.

McFLY

Unauthorized Annual 2006

Contents

McFlying High

If you don't already know who McFly are you must have been living under a rock for the past year. They are four talented lads whose infectious music has dominated the charts for most of 2004 and 2005. The boys have enjoyed more success in the last year than most musicians experience in a lifetime. Take a look at the accolades they've notched up in just one year.

MARCH 2004

- "5 Colours In Her Hair" is released and goes to number one in the charts.

JUNE 2004

- "Obviously" is released and hits number one.
- Olympic Torch Concert, London. The guys take part in a free concert to celebrate the return of the Olympic torch. They appear alongside Jamelia and Will Young at a star-studded concert in front of 77,000 people on The Mall in London. The guys perform a cover of The Beatles' hit "She Loves You".

JULY 2004

- The debut album *Room On The 3rd Floor* is released and goes to number one in the charts.
- McFly are presented with a Guinness British Hit Singles and Albums award for becoming the youngest band to ever have a number-one album, a record previously held by their idols, The Beatles.
- McFly become the first ever band to perform at a film premiere. They play three tracks at the opening of *Spiderman 2*, appearing on the rooftop of London's Leicester Square Odeon.
- Party In The Park, Hyde Park, London. The guys nearly go on stage naked after their dressing room is flooded, ruining their performing pants!

SEPTEMBER 2004

- "That Girl" is released and reaches number three in the charts.
- The band embark on their very first headlining tour, kicking off in Wolverhampton.
- McFly switch on the Christmas illuminations in Blackpool with Geri Halliwell and Lemar.
- Another gong – McFly pick up the Best Newcomer Award at the Disney Channel Kids' Awards, held at the swanky Royal Albert Hall.

FL

NOVEMBER 2004

- The single "Room On The 3rd Floor" is released and reaches number five in the charts.

DECEMBER 2004

- McFly star in a Christmas special episode of the soap *EastEnders*. They play themselves and perform a couple of songs in Albert Square. Dougie remembers, 'I wanted to nick one of Pat Butcher's earrings, but she looked too scary so I ran away!'
- McFly scoop five awards at the Smash Hits Poll Winners' Party, in London. They are voted Stars Of The Year, Best UK Band, Best Album, Best Video for "That Girl" and Danny picks up Most Fanciable Male.

JANUARY 2005

- The nominations for the Brit Awards 2005 are announced and McFly are in the running for Best Pop Act.
- The guys star in an episode of the medical drama *Casualty* as themselves. They visit a fan in hospital who has fallen from a window at their hotel. Then they find out that it is the girl's mum who is the obsessed fan.

FEBRUARY 2005

- McFly scoop a Brit Award for Best Pop Act, beating tough competition from the likes of Avril Lavigne, Westlife and Girls Aloud.
- McFly star as themselves in a Lindsay Lohan film called *Just My Luck*. They fly to Hollywood to film their scenes and contribute six songs to the soundtrack. Tom says, 'In the script I'm described as cool and remarkably talented!'

MARCH 2005

- "All About You/You've Got A Friend" is released and reaches number one.
- McFly appear in their very first TV advert. Simon Cowell played their skivvy in an ad for special editions of Walkers Crisps, in aid of Comic Relief.

What a year! And the hits just keep on coming.

I ♥ Tom

NAME:
Tom Fletcher (guitar and vocals)
DATE OF BIRTH:
17 July 1985
PLACE OF BIRTH:
Harrow
STAR SIGN:
Cancer
EYES:
Brown
SIBLINGS:
A little sister called Kerrie and an older brother called Matt

IN FIVE WORDS: 'Slightly – On – The – Fat – Side.'
LOVES: Picking his nose – especially in his sleep. Sometimes he even makes it bleed. Yuk! Oh and he really loves his Hulk T-shirt.
HATES: Football, sleeping in the dark and traffic lights.
HOBBIES: Going to the theatre. Collecting Teenage Mutant Ninja Turtles merchandise. He's been hooked on Manga comics since visiting Japan.
FAVOURITE ACTOR: Tom Hanks
FAVOURITE ACTRESS: Katie Holmes
FAVOURITE BAND: The Beach Boys
DID YOU KNOW?: Tom has a tattoo of a star on his foot. He's always in trouble with his parents. 'My mum tells me off when she see photos of me sticking my tongue out. She calls me and says, "Tom, can't you pull a normal face? Can't you smile?"'
FAVOURITE FOOD: A Twix chocolate bar
FAVOURITE SUBJECT AT SCHOOL: Art, music and science
FAVOURITE PLACE: Florida
SECRET FACT: 'I'm always crying in films. I'm a complete wuss. I watched *Love Actually* and had a lump in my throat. I also cried at *Elf*, even though it's not sad!'

I ♥ Harry

NAME:
Harry Mark Christopher Judd (drums)
NICKNAME:
Judder Harold
DATE OF BIRTH:
23 December 1985
PLACE OF BIRTH:
Chelmsford
STAR SIGN:
Capricorn
EYES:
Blue
SIBLINGS:
An older brother and an older sister

IN FIVE WORDS: 'Hairy – Scary – And – Quite – Contrary.'

LOVES: Cricket. 'I always have to watch the cricket highlights, if the Test is on. Obviously if I get the chance, I'll watch the actual cricket too.'

HATES: Computers. He's completely clueless when it comes to using a computer and barely knows how to use the Internet!

HOBBIES: Harry used to collect the backs of stickers and keep them in envelopes. He also collected fingernails. Eurgh!

FAVOURITE ACTOR: Jim Carrey

FAVOURITE ACTRESS: Jennifer Aniston

FAVOURITE BAND: The Used, Blink 182

PETS: A gerbil named Travis, a black Labrador named Percy, a Jack Russell named Tilly, five chickens and a cat named Molly.

DID YOU KNOW?: Harry's a big softie at heart. 'I'm quite broody. I just love babies and puppies and dogs. I'm such a girl like that. I just have to make a noise when I see a cute baby. I want to cuddle babies the whole time!'

FAVOURITE FOOD: Anything Italian

FAVOURITE SCHOOL SUBJECT: Art. Harry got an A* in GCSEs and also an A at AS Level for his art skills!

FAVOURITE PLACE: Barbados

SECRET FACT: Harry's rubbish at cooking. 'Microwave frankfurters are the extent of my cooking skills! I just cook for myself, I've never cooked for anyone else – well, only with the help of my mum. I won't cook for friends – no way, never will!'

I ♥ Danny

NAME:
Danny Alan David Jones (guitar and vocals)
DATE OF BIRTH:
12 March 1986
PLACE OF BIRTH:
Bolton
STAR SIGN:
Pisces
EYES:
Blue
SIBLINGS:
An older sister called Vicky

IN FIVE WORDS: 'Speed – Agility – Stamina – And – Excellence.'
LOVES: Monkeys. This year Danny got a licence to get a pet monkey to hang out with James from Busted's monkey.
HATES: Aubergines, 'I really can't see the point in them. Completely tasteless!' He also hates cats. 'They're evil.'
HOBBIES: Boxing. Danny also used to collect hubcaps off motorbikes and cars.
FAVOURITE ACTOR: Adam Sandler
FAVOURITE ACTRESS: Julia Roberts
FAVOURITE BAND: Bruce Springsteen & The E-Street Band or The Who
DID YOU KNOW?: In October 2004, Danny came third in *CosmoGirl*'s 101 Most Datable Guys poll.
FAVOURITE FOOD: Rice pudding
FAVOURITE SUBJECT AT SCHOOL: PE
FAVOURITE PLACE: Manchester and Tokyo
SECRET FACT: Danny spends the most time in front of the mirror because he has curly hair and he straightens it!

I ♥ Dougie

NAME:
Dougie Poynter (bass)
DATE OF BIRTH:
30 November 1987
PLACE OF BIRTH:
Orset
STAR SIGN:
Sagittarius
EYES:
Greeny blue
SIBLINGS:
A sister called Jazzy

IN FIVE WORDS: 'Spectacular – Fabulous – Great – Amazing – Brilliant.'
LOVES: Teenage Mutant Ninja Turtles.
HATES: The dark, fires and cooking.
HOBBIES: Dougie likes to collect Puma trainers and the keys from all the hotels the band stay in. He loves playing with his Playstation.
DID YOU KNOW?: Blue Smarties make Dougie go hyper!

FAVOURITE ACTOR: Brad Pitt
FAVOURITE ACTRESS: Hillary Duff or 'anyone fit!'
FAVOURITE BAND: Blink 182
PETS: 'I'd like a pet troll! A real live troll, please. Or a goblin – I'm not sure which. I think I'd call it Colin The Troll or Colin The Goblin. I'd get him from Narnia – I think they do mail order!'

FAVOURITE FOOD: Burritos
FAVOURITE SUBJECT AT SCHOOL: Art
FAVOURITE PLACE: California
SECRET FACT: Dougie can fold his tongue in half.

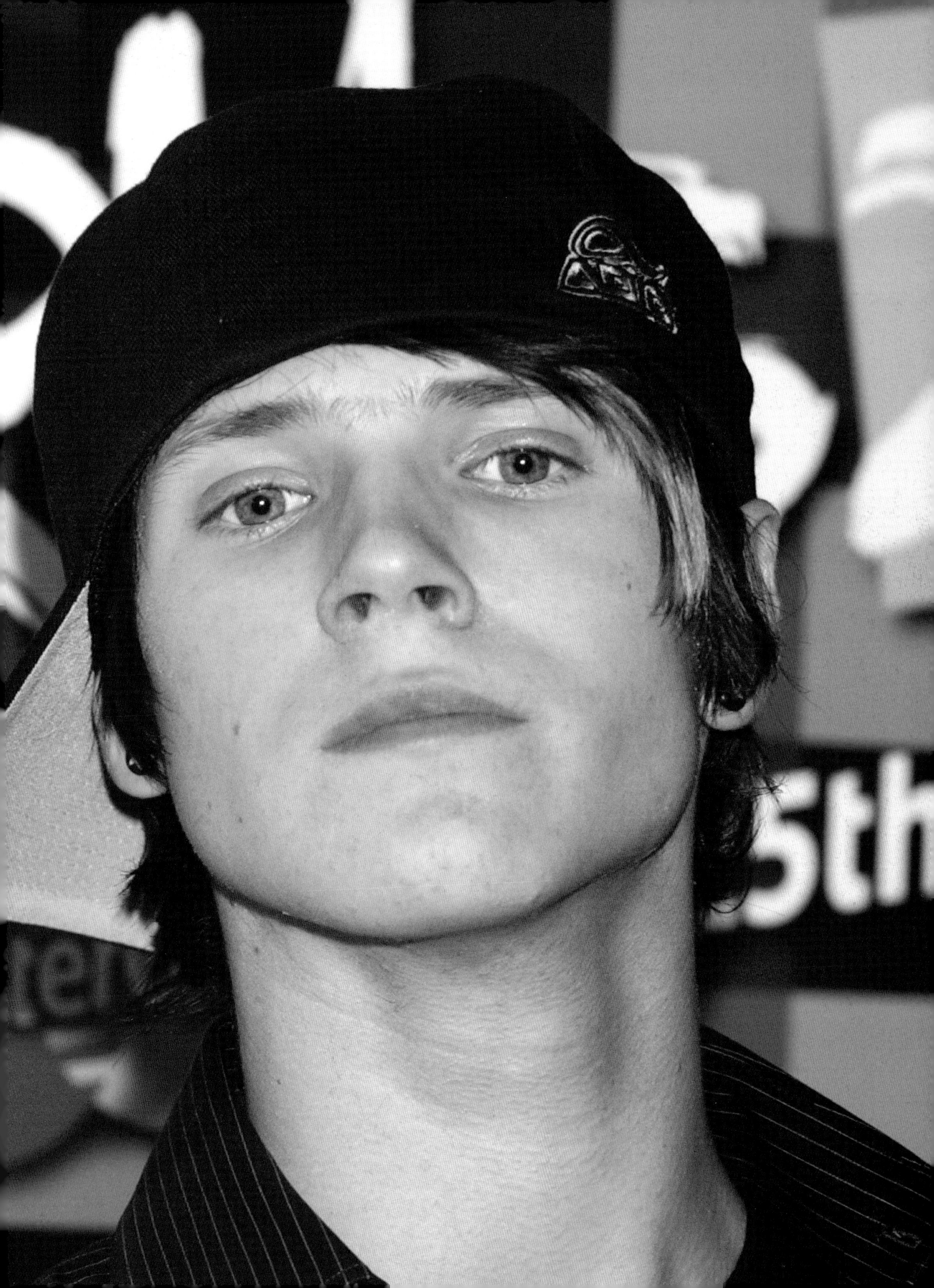

The 25th S
with Mas
The 25

with

Life In The Band

So what is life like when you are part of one of the biggest bands around? Who is the bossiest? Who is known as the diva of the group? And which McFly fella is always breaking the rules? Read on as all is revealed...

KEEPING IT REAL

Despite all their success, the guys still manage to keep their feet firmly on the ground. 'None of us are at all big-headed,' says Dougie, the youngest member of the band. 'We're exactly the same as we were before the band.' Danny agrees, 'The only thing that's changed is that my life is much more hectic now, but I get to do more things that I enjoy.'

You might be surprised to learn that the boys like to steer clear of all those showbiz bashes they get invited to too. 'We'd rather play Xbox at home than be papped at pointless celebrity parties,' says Harry. 'We're not in this for the fame.'

THE BAND RULES

Dougie: 'The rules are – there are no rules! If we had loads of piercings or something – that might be breaking some kind of rule.'

Danny: 'No, there are no rules apart from respect and don't destroy the TV! Oh and not stealing food is a rule, too. Harry goes mad! He's the munch maestro. He eats rubbish, but he doesn't know I sometimes steal it on the sly!'

Harry: 'We're not allowed to wear anything Von Dutch.'

Tom: 'We don't allow bleepish behaviour or anything. That's why Dougie's so quiet!'

BOSSY BOOTS TOM!

Danny: 'Tom thinks he's the sergeant major. He used to tell us to clean up after ourselves when we first moved in. I never did, I just ignored him!'

Tom: 'Only because the plates were going green!'

Dougie: 'The one who always has clean clothes is Tom. When the rest of us are bumming around he must go off and do it. Or maybe he has a secret cleaner we don't know about!'

TAKING ORDERS

Harry: 'We don't take to authority very well. We're quite like stroppy teenagers with attitudes, but a lot of the time we're polite.'

Danny: 'I just do them puppy eyes to get out of doing things!'

Dougie: 'I think I'm all right at taking orders. I wasn't too good at school with homework, but I never really misbehaved. I'm not very witty under pressure, so there's no point in showing myself up.'

TEMPER TANTRUMS

Dougie: 'I don't shout, but I don't like people touching my stuff. I'm quite protective over my things. I'm pretty sure Harry steals my boxers and socks! There've been a few times when I've been like "Hey, I recognize those boxers!" He doesn't wash them after either. He wears the same boxers for about four days in a row, too, so they are disgusting!'

Danny: 'Tom balloons and for no reason. You just ignore him and he goes, "You're such an idiot!" I think he's really nasty. He hurts my feelings.'

Tom: 'Dougie's just an idiot. No, he's not an idiot, but him and Danny are just a bit slow.'

Wordsearch

H	A	V	G	N	I	R	U	O	T	E	O
A	N	I	C	B	E	C	Z	E	C	R	B
R	G	U	I	T	A	R	S	A	F	E	V
P	O	L	N	D	D	U	P	D	J	H	I
H	P	Y	K	F	M	N	O	B	C	C	O
W	O	L	M	C	F	O	N	R	J	T	U
P	G	F	U	I	W	T	J	O	N	E	S
C	O	C	L	Y	O	U	U	C	R	L	L
W	I	M	L	S	D	E	R	C	A	F	Y
C	H	L	A	D	E	L	O	O	N	I	E
L	O	L	M	G	S	H	A	L	R	S	L
H	J	D	R	A	W	A	T	I	R	B	P

Can you find the following McFly words hidden in the grid? Start searching!

Guitars
Judd
Fletcher
Jones
Poynter
Broccoli
Touring
McFly
Brit Award
Hollywood
Obviously

Body Matters

Proving that girls aren't the only ones to fuss over their figures, here's the lowdown on what the McFly boys love and hate about their bodies.

TOM

LOVES: 'When I smile I have a dimple on my left cheek and I like it because it's unique.'

HATES: 'I'd like plastic surgery to reduce my nostrils and I hate my teeth, too. I always keep my mouth shut in photos. I want one of those head braces that twelve-year-olds have! I want the full scaffolding around my head. It might affect my singing, but it would be funny. Also, I hate my toe hair – there isn't very much, but it's unattractive.'

HARRY

LOVES: 'I think I've got good arms from where I drum so much. They're one of the things I wouldn't change about myself.'

HATES: 'I've got hairy feet and skinny legs and a skinny body. Sometimes, if I'm lying next to a girl, I worry that I'm smaller than her and she'll feel weird with that, but I guess she's worrying about being bigger. We worry about stuff, but at the end of the day looks aren't everything. I'm like, "Look, I really fancy you and I wouldn't be here if I didn't."'

DANNY

LOVES: 'I love my nipples – they're just the right shape.'

HATES: 'I hate my chicken legs and my freckles. I've never found anyone who shares my weird combo of ginger freckles and dark hair.'

DOUGIE

LOVES: 'I think my eyes are OK. They're really small and sometimes they completely disappear, but the girls seem to like them!'

HATES: 'My bacne. You know, acne on your back. And sometimes I get spots in random places like my chest. If I've got my top off in front of anyone, I'll cover them up with my hand as if that's how I usually sit.'

McFly Or McLie?

So you think you know all about McFly? You will do once we've sorted the facts from the fibs.

STUBBLE BREWING

The rumour: Harry wants to grow as much facial fuzz as Santa Claus.

Fact or Fib: Fact.

Harry: 'I just can't be bothered shaving. If anything, my all-time beardy hero is Clint Eastwood – he had some amazing stubble.'

EASTENDER

The rumour: Tom auditioned for a role in *EastEnders*.

Fact or Fib: Fib.

Tom: 'Not true, but once I appeared as an extra. I also once auditioned for the part of Anakin Skywalker in *Star Wars Episode I – The Phantom Menace*. I nearly got it, but I was a bit too old. And I appear in the choir on the new remixed DVD soundtrack of *Return Of The Jedi*.'

DERANGED DOUGIE

The rumour: Dougie is officially bonkers!

Fact or Fib: Fact.

Tom: 'Dougie is a bit of a weirdo. It's the quiet ones you've gotta watch!'

MOTOR MANIA

The rumour: Tom bought his parents a car after signing a £3 million record deal.

Fact or Fib: Fib.

Tom: 'My mum doesn't even drive! She laughed her head off when she heard that story.'

Dougie: 'We didn't sign our record deal for £3 million. It was more like £1 million.'

BUM NOTES
The rumour: McFly like to pinch girls' bums.
Fact or Fib: Fact.
Danny: 'I love a good bum. The actress Kate Beckinsale has an amazing one. I love looking at them from afar.'

McFRIENDLESS
The rumour: McFly are gutted they're not invited to any showbiz bashes.
Fact or Fib: Fact.
Danny: 'It's disgraceful! We never get invited anywhere! People probably think we're too young. I'd love to go to a Christina or Britney party with loads of fit girls, but it'll never happen.'

POYNTER'S PUKEFEST
The rumour: Dougie was so nervous at the McFly auditions that he actually barfed.
Fact or Fib: Fact.
Dougie: 'I was petrified that day. I remember walking into the room and throwing up in a bin. Sometimes I'm still sick after gigs if I drink too much coffee.'
Danny: 'Dougie used to pass out if he got nervous. I'd shout 'WOAH! Watch out for Dougie!'

R.I.P. BUFFY
The rumour: Dougie mourned the loss of his pet lizard, Buffy, by holding a funeral.
Fact or Fib: Fib.
Dougie: 'Sadly Buffy did die last summer. It was old age. I was gutted, but I didn't hold a funeral! We buried her in my friend's garden and got a gravestone for her. She's in lizard heaven now.'

EPSI PRESENTS
HRISTMA
Atticu

2004

Video Diary

Track: **"Room On The 3rd Floor"**
Location: **Black Island Studios, Acton, West London**
Start Time: **7am**
Finish: **1am**

The McFly boys star as figurines from a scale-model kit that come to life. For the video they had to be painted top to toe in blue paint.

Tom: 'In the video, we're little models, like Airfix kits, and all the parts of our body come to life. So our hands start strumming guitars while they're separate from our body. It's really cool.'
Harry: 'We were painted blue and there was a blank screen behind us so they could do loads of animated stuff with it later on. The blue paint was gross. I felt like a Smurf.'
Danny: 'The paint had glue in it so it dried hard and glossy. It took me about seventeen showers just to get it off!'
Tom: 'At one point they told Dougie he was finished and that he could take all the blue paint off, but after he scrubbed it off, they made him put it all on again. They'd forgotten he had to shoot another scene! He was gutted!'
Danny: 'We were making fun of each other all day. I took loads of photos on my phone.'
Tom: 'Our heads were clamped still and there's one point where my whole body was clamped to this stand – it was like body scaffolding. Weird!'
Dougie: 'We couldn't itch our faces, pick our noses or bite our fingernails... there was no chance of snogging either. The paint was really irritating as well. It made me go all sweaty and sticky – yuck!'
Danny: 'Me and Tom had to wear hairnets – well, I used the bottom of some tights! I've never worn tights before.'
Dougie: 'I thought my hairgrips were cool. It's a new look I was trying to work, but I don't think it's going to catch on!'

96
TRENT
FM

Hearts Of Gold

After their rollercoaster ride to fame, the boys were keen to give something back. So when the chance to get involved in Red Nose Day came their way, they grabbed it.

McFly recorded 2005's official Red Nose Day single. The track, "All About You" written by Tom, was recorded at the famous Abbey Road studios. Released on 7 March, it was part of a double-A-side with a cover of "You've Got A Friend". A sixty-piece orchestra crammed into the studio to record the anthem, and the video featured a host of famous faces including Johnny Vegas, Dermot O'Leary, Davina McCall, Kate Thornton, Graham Norton, Fearne Cotton and Ruby Wax. As part of the campaign, the band paid a visit to Uganda in Africa and here they recall that emotional trip.

Tom: 'We expected it to be unpleasant, but it was an amazing place. We went to Kamwokya Christian Caring Community that benefited from the money Comic Relief raised last year.'

Harry: 'It was a very poor place with mud huts, but at the same time it was only five minutes away from the main city, so it was quite surreal.'

Danny: 'I was totally shell-shocked. Like, all the sights and smells there were so bad. But at the same time it was quite uplifting. When we left I was crying – it was all so emotional.'

Dougie: 'But we had a real laugh with all the kids. They picked me up and carried me about – luckily they didn't drop me. They tried to carry me away!'

Harry: 'We had a piggyback race which I won! And we were playing loads of games, running around and stuff. We actually had quite a laugh, which you might not expect.'

Danny: 'The kids were hanging off us. One girl was stroking my legs and trying to pick my tattoo off! But you'd lift one kid up and another one would go "Me! Me!" Lifting everyone was like a work-out! It was brilliant!'

Harry: 'We made our video in a local square. Afterwards the kids put on their national costumes and got us to join in their dance. I danced with this amazing deaf and dumb kid who must have felt the beats through the ground.'

Shhhh... Secrets!

Don't tell anyone, but here's a bumper selection of McFly secrets for you...

- Harry hates gardening. He says, 'It's for old people!'
- Danny used only to eat tomato ketchup sandwiches. Eurgh!
- Harry got his tongue pierced in December 2004. 'It was really sore. I was supposed to put ice on it just after I'd had it done, to keep the swelling down. The trouble is, my teeth are so sensitive that I can't keep ice in my mouth long enough!'
- Tom is a secret scab eater. 'Knee scabs are much tastier than elbow scabs – elbow scabs have usually been exposed way too much.'
- Dougie is very ticklish especially on his bum and left knee. 'My left knee is much more ticklish than my right.'
- Danny is obsessed with chocolate éclairs.
- According to Tom, 'Harry has fingers for toes! He can pick things up with his feet.'
- Danny got his first guitar when he was eight years old for Christmas from his parents.
- If Dougie was a girl for the day he'd get his nails done.
- Harry confesses that when he was younger, his sister used to make him cry during rows.
- Dougie once put a piece of sweetcorn up his nose. Bogey-licious!
- Danny's worst fashion mistake was at the band's first photoshoot. He says he had on a really 'bad baseball jacket'.
- Tom annoys the group by always making them turn off their mobiles.

- Harry's the only member of McFly who can grow facial hair.
- Tom's convinced that when people die they go into space.
- The boys have a rule to try to eat one piece of unusual fruit a day.
- Once Tom made his sister some burgers, but accidentally set them on fire.
- Tom doesn't have a bedroom door. Instead he's got some bright orange blinds.
- Harry once had to have twenty-six stitches after he ran into an open window and cut his head.
- Dougie has always wanted to bathe in baked beans.
- Harry has won table-tennis championships.
- Danny and Harry have both milked a goat.
- If Harry's angry he curls up in a ball and screams all his anger out.
- The McFly boys all hate Valentine's Day, apart from romantic Dougie.
- Harry only washes his hair once every three or four weeks.
- Tom's parents bought him a car for his seventeenth birthday.
- Tom and Dougie are addicted to a *Star Wars* game on Playstation 2.
- Danny's the bravest member of the band. 'I saved someone's life on the Tube. The door shut on a woman's head and I prised it open, but she wasn't very grateful!'

- The McFly boys have a cleaner called Dorita, who also cooks for the lads. The lads call her 'Doritos'!
- Danny and Harry run away screaming if they see wasps.
- McFly have been inspired by some rather strange people. On their album, Tom thanks the Teenage Mutant Ninja Turtles for being an inspiration to him!
- Danny flew to the Caribbean for his Christmas holidays, and on the way back the air hostess recognized him and upgraded him and his family to first class!
- Tom used to be bullied at school. 'I went to a theatre school and the local kids were nasty to me about it. It was hard.'
- Last Christmas Tom jetted off to New York, where he went to lots of basketball games.
- Danny says he likes to wear his fringe long to cover his ugly face.
- Harry owns a pair of wild leopard-print underwear! 'They're long johns in fact. Mmmm, leopard-print long johns. The good thing about them is that they're really tight – grrrr!'
- When Tom first started going to school and getting trains into London on his own, his Nan would follow him to make sure he was OK.
- Danny's favourite pudding is rice pudding.
- Tom would love to meet Paul McCartney and Green Day, although he says, 'I don't think I'd know what to say to them because I'd be too star-struck!'
- Harry used to have a comfort blanket called 'Dar' when he was younger.
- If Dougie could invite three people to a dinner he'd ask Tom Delonge from Blink 182, Jennifer Aniston and Har Mar Superstar.
- Danny used to be in a band called Y2K with his sister.
- Dougie's nickname at school was Grunger.
- Tom collects comedy pants. 'I've got some Snow White socks and pants – they match! My mum got them for me.'
- Danny always tries to steal clothes from stylists at photoshoots. 'I just wear them and try to walk out!'
- Dougie's nickname for his mum is Mother Goose.
- Tom once appeared in a TV commercial for Curry's.
- Harry used to work in a salmon factory over the school holidays to earn extra money.
- Tom gets really ill if he eats prawns.
- Harry's dad used to call him Dinky because he was tiny.

The Girl Zone

The fab four 'fess up to their love-life likes and dislikes.

DATING DISASTERS

Well, everyone has had dating disasters, even the boys from McFly.

Danny: 'I once dated a girl who stank the whole room out. I thought I'd give her a chance – maybe she could suck on some spearmint or chew some gum. But no, it was deep down stinky breath, and you can't get rid of that!'

Dougie: 'All of my dates end in disaster because I get tongue-tied and I mix my words up and everything comes out wrong. I get really nervous eating in front of girls because I don't have very good table manners. Once I was on a date and it was just like *Titanic* – I had no idea what cutlery to use. I looked especially silly in front of my date when I picked up the wrong spoon for the starter.'

Tom: 'I had an Italian girlfriend when I was at school. One night I went to her house for dinner and her gran cooked us some food that was so spicy I started burning up. Sweat was literally dripping off me – it was terrible!'

Harry: 'I went on a double date and the girl I was with got her friend to tell me I was dumped! We were only halfway through the day and still had to spend the rest of it together. It was really harsh!'

Harry: 'I once met a girl on holiday and she was gorgeous. I thought I had no chance, but she told me on the last day that she fancied me. I got her number and went to stay at her house for two days – which was very brave of me as I was only fourteen. I'd only had one other girlfriend and was still at the stage where I would talk to girls and get really nervous. It was awkward at first. We knew we liked each other, but didn't really do anything. She didn't know what we should talk about, so she just took the mick out of me – it was out of order! Then her friend came over and was like, "What are you doing? She likes you!" Then she showed me text messages saying stuff about me that was really good! I was like, "What? She's been rinsing me all day!" So when she came back in the room, I told her to sit next to me and I held her hand. We only kissed once though. I was really pleased to get out of there!'

GIRL TURN-OFFS

Want to know how to impress a McFlyer? Just take note of the following dos and don'ts and you'll be fine...

Tom: 'I like girls who are really brown with a suntan. But I hate it when you get off the phone with a girl and they text you immediately and expect to carry on chatting via text. And I hate it when a girl phones you and says, "Oh can you phone me back 'cause of my phone bill?" Well what about MY phone bill?! And I think muscular armpits are a real turn-off. That's the least attractive part of a girl's body.'

Danny: 'I don't hate anything about girls. I love all of them! I like girls that shout and dance around a lot, and girls with curvy bodies and lovely smiles.'

Dougie: 'I hate it when girls wear too much make-up or when they get fussy about stuff. Why can't they just chill out?'

Harry: 'I hate it when girls try to be cool and impress me instead of just being themselves. I also think that farting is a bit off-putting.'

LOVE BITES

Harry: 'I've given myself a love bite before, just to see if it worked.'

Dougie: 'I'm not really into love bites. If a girl tried to give me one, I'd be like, "What are you doing to my neck?!"'

Danny: 'I've never received a proper love bite and I don't want to either – I think they're disgusting! A girl gave me a tiny one on my belly once for a joke. I hated it!'

Tom: 'My ex-girlfriend gave me a love bite. I thought it was quite cool, but slightly weird. No one noticed it, so I didn't have to walk around wearing a polo neck.'

Real-Life Romeos

The McFly boys get in touch with their romantic side. These boys certainly know how to sweep a girl off her feet.

Tom: 'I'd pick true love over fame. I love being in a band, but the fame side isn't all it's cracked up to be.'

Dougie: 'I'm terrible around girls. I totally clam up and don't know what to say and I feel like I'm just watching what's happening, I can't control it. I've never been anyone's boyfriend, but I reckon I'd be good because I don't mind being romantic and buying a girl flowers. I think I could sweep her off her feet!'

Danny: 'I need girls to spell it out for me. I can never tell if a girl likes me.'

Harry: 'I treat girls really well. I always make sure I buy her flowers. It's the done thing. I took a rose round to a girl's house in the middle of the night once as a surprise. But she told me to come back in the morning!'

Tom: 'I once wrote a song as a Valentine's Day present for a girl.'

Danny: 'The most romantic thing you could do is make out under the stars.'

Dougie: 'The most romantic thing I've done is light candles round the house for a girl.'

Harry: 'I've written a song for a girl before. I never gave it to her – it's too personal. And, no, it's not on the next McFly album!'

Tom: 'The most romantic thing I did for a girl was post a note through her letterbox for when she moved in, and I've bought flowers for girls a few times.'

Danny: 'I once made a cup of tea for a girl. I think that's quite romantic!'

Harry: 'I can be quite romantic at times, but I've never done the candlelit dinner thing. I think I'm very much the proper gent though.'

Famous Fancies

Everyone has a crush on someone famous, but which celebrity ladies catch McFly's wandering eyes?

Danny: 'I wouldn't mind some JLo but I know I've got no chance! But I fancy Joss Stone too, and she's the same age as me so maybe I've got a chance with her.'
Dougie: 'I fancy all of Girls Aloud – even Nicola.'
Tom: 'I've got a bit of a thing for Paris Hilton, but I'm in love with Katie Holmes too.'
Harry: 'I'm so in love with Angelina Jolie, Keira Knightley and Rachel Stevens. I shouted to Rachel at Party In The Park last year. She didn't turn around. I said "Hello", trying to play it cool, but she completely blanked me. I was gutted. But I walked past Avril Lavigne once and nodded. She nodded back!'

THE PERFECT DATE

Tom: 'I'd like to go to the cinema in Times Square in New York.'
Danny: 'I like to take girls to gigs and restaurants. There's nothing more romantic than taking a girl to a sit-down meal at an Italian restaurant, and if you both have garlic bread you'll be ok. But if just one of you eats it, it's not good!
Dougie: 'I'd like to spend the day at San Diego Zoo. I love animals and I hope my date would too!'
Harry: 'I'd whisk my date off to a beautiful island and we'd snog underneath a coconut tree. But usually I like taking girls to the cinema, then you can maybe hold hands.'

CHAT-UP LINES

Tom: 'The best way for a girl to chat me up is to say, "Hi, I want to pull you!" That's never happened to me yet though. But if I want to find out about a girl I like, I just ask her friends. I'm not so good at talking to girls, so I try to make friends with her mates first.'
Harry: 'I don't think I've ever been chatted up before, I don't believe in them. The best way would be for a girl to talk to me and be natural. I give girls I like a knowing look and a smile. Nothing too cheesy though.'
Dougie: 'I never chat up girls. I wait for them to come to me.'
Danny: 'Sometimes I get shy when I ask a girl out. I can talk to girls normally, but not actually ask the question. Sometimes I just go for it.'

Pucker Up

McFly reveal their smooching styles and how and where they liked to be kissed!

DANNY

- 'I had my first kiss in Year 6 with a girl called Chelsea. We used to have kissing competitions so I knew what I was doing. We'd have timed contests to see who could kiss the longest. My record was half an hour!'
- 'This one girl called Lucy pushed me inside a school locker and snogged me silly! She was the best snog I've had in my life – twelve out of ten. Lovely!'
- 'I love having my ears kissed and I love to suck lips!'

HARRY

- 'I like to be kissed on my ear and on my bum cheek!'
- 'This girl was trying to kiss me, but I just didn't fancy her so I told her I had a girlfriend. Then I had to have a whole conversation with her about my imaginary girlfriend.
- 'I remember my first kiss. It was messy, but it was my first kiss so I didn't really know what I was doing. It was a bit slobbery, but I loved it. I'd been dreaming of that moment for ages.'
- 'The most number of girls I've snogged in one night is eight! I was on a roll!'
- 'Not too much tongue is the key to a good kiss!'

DOUGIE

- 'A girl licked my face once and that was amazing!'
- 'I've never had any complaints when it comes to kissing so I must be pretty good.'

TOM

- 'I once snogged four girls in the same night!'
- 'Once when I was younger, I was playing spin the bottle. I kissed this girl and it was like she was eating my face! It was really bad; I actually ended up with a wet nose.'
- 'A good kisser is someone who doesn't ram her tongue down your throat and isn't sloppy.'
- 'My favourite snog was when I kissed a girl in a park, when we were hiding in the bushes – that was a cool moment.'
- 'I'm an amazing kisser. I'm ten out of ten, definitely!'
- 'I'm really ticklish, but I like my ear being nibbled and I like being kissed on my bottom lip.'

On Tour

Get a peek at what life is like for McFly on tour as we grab our passes and go backstage.

GAME FOR A LAUGH

During their spare time while they're waiting around in their dressing room before a performance, McFly use a very special technique to warm up – a game of Twister. 'Sometimes we get so bored backstage we have grape fights!' confesses Danny.

The McFly boys love their toys and count them as their backstage essentials. The lads always ask for an X–box, four controllers and lots of sweeties to keep them amused.

ON THE ROAD

Dougie admits, 'We don't do laundry on tour, instead we just bring a different set of clothes for each day.'

Tom is strict when it comes to timekeeping. 'We have curfews when we're on the road and we've broken them a few times, but we're not silly. If we've got to be up at 5am we'll make sure we get enough sleep.' But that still doesn't stop Harry from always being the last one to wake up, and he's always late to arrive.

There's only one rule on the tour bus. And what is it? 'We're not allowed to do number twos on the tour bus!' says Danny. 'This one time, Tom was dying to do a poo, but he had to wait about an hour until we got to a service station. His face was going all red!'

WHAT A LOAD OF PANTS!

Ever wondered what the lads do with the underwear their fans throw at them on stage? Are you sure you want to know?

Harry: 'I remember this one time Dougie wore black lace knickers with a bobble on the back! It all started because Danny was downstairs with a girl and we decided to wear the knickers fans sent us. So we just walked into the room wearing them. Then, when Danny and the girl started laughing at us, we danced around in the knickers. That was a one-off though. We were in a really immature and hyperactive mood at the time.'

Tom: 'Those knickers were really weird though. They go right up your bum!'

Disney
CHANNEL
KIDS awards
Disney
CHANNEL
KIDS AWARDS

Disney
KIDS AWARDS

The Real Deal

McFly love mischief; they must be the cheekiest boys in pop. Here's what they really get up to.

HOUSE PARTIES

The lads love mad McFly house parties. Here's what happens...

Danny: 'We get our bums out!'

Dougie: 'Tom plays the piano and we throw stuff at each other.'

Danny: 'And we fall down stairs!'

Harry: 'One time we moved everything around in each other's bedrooms as well!'

PRACTICAL JOKES

Tom: 'When we were in America, the guys told the waiter it was my birthday and he brought over a huge cake. It wasn't my birthday at all and I was so embarrassed!'

Danny: 'I like slapping Dougie when he's asleep. It's funny!'

Harry: 'Tom once woke me up by whacking one of my drums next to my ear – it really hurt!'

Tom: 'I used to put dirty socks inside their pillow cases so they couldn't work out what the smell was!'

DARES

Tom: 'I dared Danny to let me shoot him with a paintball gun at like, point-blank range. And he let me! I had to persuade him and then I said, "If you don't let me, then I'll shoot you anyway." So he did. He had a big bruise!'

Dougie: 'The other boys dare me to dress up in girls' stuff, but they don't need to because I absolutely love it!'

Dougie: 'I'd run down the street completely naked for a bag of chips and a snog!'

CLASSROOM ANTICS

Tom: 'I cut my finger with a scalpel and it just went splssssh with loads of blood. It stained the science room floor and they had to get a new floor put in.'

Harry: 'One Sports Day I was so nervous I wet myself! I was only ten and it was only a tiny dribble. Only I noticed it!'

Dougie: 'I wasn't naughty, but I never did my homework. I used to come up with very lame excuses like "Sorry it's not in, but I witnessed an accident this morning and the police took my homework away as evidence!"'

MONKEYING AROUND

Harry: 'Well, I like messing around, but we're all totally bananas! We're always doing stupid voices and talking about mad things. I guess Dougie and me are the cheekiest though.'
Tom: 'We're all pretty funny, but Dougie's always monkeying around. He's a real joker! He does and says silly things.'
Harry: 'I went on a school trip a few years ago to Switzerland. We had a brilliant time, but one night at the hotel a party in my room got out of hand and the other guests complained to our teachers about the noise. To teach me a lesson, I was banned from skiing the following day, which was actually great because I was tired after the party anyway!'

GETTING NAKED

Harry: 'I've worn Speedos on the beach for a joke when I've been with friends!'
Dougie: 'I went on this cruise at Christmas and one night I was hanging out with some mates I'd made on the ship, when we saw some people in the hot tub – naked!'
Harry: 'This one time we saw a guy getting changed in the house opposite ours. He was wearing Y-fronts and checked out his muscles in the mirror. It was so funny!'
Tom: 'I've never been naked in public before, but I've walked around the house naked for a joke.'

BAD HABITS

Danny: 'I'm always catching farts and throwing them at people. I do it to Dougie.'
Harry: 'Danny makes an irritating gulping sound when he sleeps.'
Tom: 'Harry takes about seven hours to eat a meal.'
Danny: 'Tom's nose-picking has got to be the grossest habit.'
Dougie: 'My bad habits are not cutting my toenails, not washing my hair and eating dead skin. When I went on holiday with Tom and James from Busted, I ate the layers of skin that were peeling from James's sunburnt back!'
Harry: 'I always bite my nails and pick spots.'

67
ZERO

The Fans

If there's one thing McFly can always count on, it's their devoted fans. This is what they have to say about you lot...

Danny: 'Our fans are the best. They always give us loads of presents. This one time, I said in an interview that I liked cakes and suddenly girls started giving them to me!'

Tom: 'Some fans are a bit extreme. I mean we've had some girls ask if they can spend the night in our room with us! And we've all had marriage proposals too, but it's hard knowing what to say!'

Harry: 'I think I treat our fans well, but I usually give a little bit extra to the ones who come from different countries or travel a long way to see us.'

Danny: 'I'd totally snog a fan if she was fit. I'd have no problems locking lips with her!'

Harry: 'I'd snog a fan, I look forward to it one day and I'd definitely date a girl who loved our music. But I'd draw the line at a screaming psycho!'

Tom: 'Danny always hands out his mobile number to our fans. At least a thousand girls must have his digits!'

Danny: 'Dougie has a blabber mouth, he always spills our secrets, especially in front of our fans.'

Tom: 'Yeah, when it was still a secret that we were going to Africa for Comic Relief we weren't supposed to tell anyone, but the fans asked what we were up to and he blabbed. He always does stuff like that!'

Danny: 'I was on my way home, when my cab driver said he wanted an autograph for his eight-year-old daughter. I asked him where she lived and he said it was kind of on the way, so we did a detour to their house and I met her! I went fifteen minutes out of my way just to say hello.'

Harry: 'Sometimes fans ask me for a spare bracelet and if I've got one I'll give it to them. They give us so much all the time with their support, the least I can do is give them my bracelet!'

Questions, Questions

All your questions answered:

What are McFly's top five films?

1. *The Goonies*
2. *Forrest Gump*
3. *The Shawshank Redemption*
4. *Gremlins 2*
5. *Back To The Future*

What are Dougie's top five musical instruments?

1. Bass guitar
2. Drums
3. Piano
4. Guitar
5. Fiddle

What are McFly's top five favourite albums?

1. Counting Crows – *August And Everything After*. 'I became obsessed with it and had it on repeat for a year,' says Harry.
2. The Beatles – *With The Beatles.* 'There's not one bad song on this record. It's my favourite album of all time,' says Tom.
3. The Used – *Used.* 'It reminds me of a school trip to Greece, when I first heard it,' says Harry.
4. Bruce Springsteen – *Live In New York City*. 'My mum got me hooked on Bruce,' remembers Danny.
5. Led Zeppelin – *How The West Was Won (Live)*. 'It's just an amazing record,' raves Dougie.

What do you listen to if you're feeling happy?

Harry: 'Any Reel Big Fish song.'
Danny: '"All My Loving" by The Beatles.'
Dougie: '"Starting Line".'

...if you're feeling angry?

Dougie: 'Anything by Thursday.'
Harry: 'The Used.'
Danny: 'Bruce Springsteen – he's an all rounder.'

...if you're in the party mood?

Danny: 'Oasis.'
Harry: 'Red Hot Chili Peppers.'
Tom: '"I Get Around" by The Beach Boys.'

...if you're feeling heartbroken?

Danny: 'The soundtrack to *Blood Brothers*.'
Harry: 'Counting Crows.'
Tom: '"Yesterday" by The Beatles.'

Which superhero would you be?

Harry: 'I'd be Marmite Man, with the special power of being able to eat Marmite whenever I wanted.'

Danny: 'I'd shrink to the size of a rat to run away from tricky situations. I'd be called Rat Man.'

Tom: 'Super Boobie would be a cool action hero. When someone cheesed me off, my boobs would expand to whack them in the face.'

How would McFly spend the perfect afternoon?

Dougie: 'I'd clean myself all over.'

Tom: 'Visit my family who are all off work ill.'

Harry: 'Go for a walk, read a book, meditate – be at one with myself.'

Dany: 'Go to the pub!'

If a film was made of your life, who would play you?

Dougie: 'Kevin Spacey, it would be a historic epic like *Alexander*.'

Tom: 'Tom Hanks and it would be a continuation of the *Star Wars* films.'

Harry: 'A sly fox...'

Danny: 'George Clooney, I reckon.'

Who would be your dream person to duet with?

Danny: 'I'd love to do anything with the Gallagher brothers or Brian McFadden.'

Harry: 'Paul McCartney.'

Tom: 'I'd love to write with someone like Brian Wilson – that'd be amazing.'

What are your phobias?

Dougie: 'I don't like fire – it burns!'

Harry: 'Flying freaks me out a bit.'

Tom: 'I'm still afraid of the dark.'

What was the first record you bought?

Harry: 'I think it was Oasis. The first single I bought was "Stand By Me" and their album *What's The Story Morning Glory?*'

Dougie: 'I was given my first album by my auntie. *Enema Of The State* by Blink 182.'

Tom: 'Mine was the Spice Girls' album!'

What is the most embarrassing record you own?

Harry: 'I've got an album by Simply Red, but I quite like it!'

Tom: 'I've got a *Dawson's Creek* album which is pretty cringey, but I like the songs on it.'

Danny: '*The Very Best Of Michael McDonald* is lurking somewhere in my collection.'

A Bumper Quiz

Test your knowledge with this tougher-than-tough bumper McFly quiz. Look out, not all the answers are in this book!

TRICKY TEASERS

1. What was McFly's first number one single?
A. "Obviously"
B. "5 Colours In Her Hair"
C. "Room On The 3rd Floor"

2. Which member of McFly co-wrote Busted's second album?
A. Tom
B. Harry
C. Danny

3. A character from which film gave the band its name?
A. *Shrek*
B. *Mean Girls*
C. *Back To The Future*

4. At which prestigious awards ceremony did McFly pick up the gong for Best Pop Act?
A. The Disney Kids Awards
B. The Smash Hits Poll Winners' Party
C. The Brit Awards

5. Which celeb appeared as McFly's scivvy in a crisps advert?
A. Simon Cowell
B. Cat Deeley
C. Ant and Dec

TRUE OR FALSE?

1. Tom absolutely hates football.
2. Danny has four sisters.
3. Harry is a trained ballet dancer.
4. Tom once peed in a public swimming pool.
5. Dougie always uses cheesy chat-up lines on girls.
6. Danny fancies Joss Stone.
7. Harry's afraid of the dark.
8. Dougie has always wanted a pet troll.
9. Tom has a tattoo of a guitar on his foot.
10. Danny was born in Manchester.

GUESS WHOSE HOBBY?

1. Playing Playstation
2. Cricket
3. Going to the theatre
4. Boxing

BEDROOM BITS

If you were to find these items, in whose bedroom are you most likely to be?

1. A signed Bruce Springsteen poster
2. A Hulk T-shirt
3. The skin of a lizard
4. Cuddly toys

ANSWERS

TRICKY TEASERS

1. B, 2. A, 3. C, 4. C, 5. A

TRUE OR FALSE?

1. True
2. False
3. False
4. True
5. False
6. True
7. True
8. True
9. False
10. False

GUESS WHOSE HOBBY?

1. Dougie
2. Harry
3. Tom
4. Danny

BEDROOM BITS

1. Danny's
2. Tom's
3. Dougie's
4. Harry's

HOW DID YOU DO?

0 – 9
McClueless
You do know this book is about a band called McFly, right? With this kind of low score we doubt it. You seem to be vaguely aware of our favourite fab four and what they look like, but that's about it! Grab a copy of their album *Room On The 3rd Floor* and get clued up.

10 – 17
McAverage
You might be mad for McFly but there's still room for improvement. Sure you've taped all their TV appearances, read loads of their interviews and got all the CDs, but you require just a little bit more dedication.

18 – 27
McFanatic
Congratulations. With this kind of scorching score it's clear that you're a McFly maniac. You probably know more about the band than the boys do themselves and there's nothing the lads do that you don't see. Erm, actually, are you sure you're not in the band?